YOUR LAND
AND
MY LAND
The Middle
East

We Visit

TURKEY

Amelia

Mitchell Lane
PUBLISHERS
P.O. Box 196
Hockessin, Delaware 19707

YOUR LAND AND MY LAND

The Middle East

Afghanistan
Iran
Iraq
Israel
Kuwait
Oman
Pakistan
Saudi Arabia
Turkey
Yemen

Kirkuk

ZAGROS MOUNTA

Qom

Arāk

Kermānshāh

Baghdad

Esfahān

IRAQ

IRAN

YOUR LAND
AND
MY LAND
The Middle
East

We Visit

TURKEY

Sanaa

YEMEN

ydah

Al Mukallā

Arabia

tasco

Printing   1   2   3   4   5   6   7   8   9

Special thanks to Ercüment and Kayleigh Arslan for sharing their thoughts about Turkey and their revani recipe.

Library of Congress Cataloging-in-Publication Data
LaRoche, Amelia.
  We visit Turkey / by Amelia LaRoche.
      p. cm. — (Your land and my land: the Middle East)
  Includes bibliographical references and index.
  ISBN 978-1-58415-956-8 (library bound)
  1. Turkey—Juvenile literature. I. Title.
  DR417.4.L37 2011
   6.1 2—dc95
                                                                              2011030765

eBook ISBN: 9781612280967

PUBLISHER'S NOTE: This story is based on the author's extensive research, which she believes to be accurate. Documentation of this research is on page 61.

    The Internet sites referenced herein were active as of the publication date. Due to the fleeting nature of some web sites, we cannot guarantee they will all be active when you are reading this book.

    To reflect current usage, we have chosen to use the secular era designations BCE ("before the common era") and CE ("of the common era") instead of the traditional designations BC ("before Christ") and AD (*anno Domini,* "in the year of the Lord").

Contents

The Grand Bazaar in Istanbul is Turkey's largest covered market. Over a quarter million people visit daily.

Introduction

Where is the Middle East? *What* is the Middle East? And is Turkey part of it? These seem like simple questions—until you start asking them. An executive at an oil company might not give the same answer as a history professor at a Turkish university. Many Westerners have heard newscasters talk about war and peace in the Middle East, but they still don't know much about this region.

The term *Middle East* was invented about a hundred years ago, but not by the people who lived there. Military men in England and the United States used it to describe a region on their charts.[1]

The entire Asian continent has been called the East—by people living to its west. They once called China and eastern Russia the Far East. They called closer parts, including Turkey, the Near East. These terms are mostly used in a historical way now.

Today it is generally accepted that the Middle East is the part of Asia where it meets Europe and Africa. Some people consider these countries to be part of the Middle East: Turkey, Armenia, Azerbaijan, Bahrain, Georgia, Iran, Iraq, Israel, Jordan, Kuwait, Lebanon, Oman, Qatar, Saudi Arabia,

Syria, the United Arab Emirates, and Yemen. Other people say parts of North Africa, including Egypt, should also be considered as part of the Middle East. Still others argue that Armenia, Azerbaijan, Georgia, and Turkey are part of Europe.

The countries in the Middle East are as diverse as the countries of Europe or North America. Turkey is no more like Iran than France is like Italy or the United States is like Mexico. They may share certain characteristics and even borders, but they have traits that make them as unique as any two families who live next door to each other.

Today Turkey has ties with its Middle Eastern *and* European neighbors. Its ability to get along with both will be carefully watched by the rest of the world in the coming decades.

Cappadocia is a region in central Turkey whose "fairy chimneys" were made by volcanic eruptions millions of years ago, then carved by wind and rain. As early as the third century, Christians fleeing Roman soldiers tunneled hidden cities several stories down into the soft rock. People still live in some of the hollowed-out houses. Balloon rides from Göreme are a popular way to see the moonlike landscape.

A Rich Blend

Turkey is a blend of old and new, and of east and west. In its sparkling cities, young office workers in miniskirts share sidewalks with elderly ladies in headscarves. Groups of men gather to drink tea and share news as they have for centuries, only now they do it outside cafés that offer Internet access. Ancient mosques sit blocks from skyscrapers with luxury penthouses. In this religious country where almost everyone is a Muslim, the government and laws are secular—they are not based on religion.

The face of Turkey is changing fast. People are flooding out of its mountain villages and into its fast-growing cities, or to other countries altogether. Wherever they land, Turks remember their roots, and identify themselves by the village where they were born—even if they never go back.

Turkey's people are young—nearly 95 percent of them are under the age of sixty-five.[1] Respect for the elderly is still important, but some of those elders complain that the Internet and television are eroding family values. Children are adored. One travel writer remembers getting on a bus in the Turkish countryside and watching as a baby was handed from passenger to passenger to be held and kissed by strangers.[2]

This gem of a country is like a huge outdoor museum. Its land is dotted with the stony ruins of civilizations that have risen and fallen over thousands of years. It is the site of one of the world's first cities, and it was the last home of the Virgin Mary. It has hundreds of miles

A Turkish woman spins yarn for a kilim

FYI FACT: It makes sense that birds called turkeys would be from Turkey, but they're not—they're from the Americas. Nobody knows how these winged creatures get their name, but one story says it was a case of mistaken identity. When Spanish explorers brought turkeys to England, the English mistook them for another type of bird they'd already named "turkey," after the Turkish traders who first brought it. That bird wasn't from Turkey, either. It was an African species.

of white sand beaches; quaint villages where colorful Turkish carpets, called kilims, are woven by hand; orchards where most of the world's hazelnuts are grown; and majestic mountains, including Ararat, where legend says Noah's ark came to rest after the flood.

Its warm people, beautiful and varied landscapes, and rich history make it a special place to live. *"Ne mutlu Türküm diyene!"* or "Happy is the person who can say, 'I am a Turk!' " is a common phrase. No wonder Turkey is so popular with tourists. More than 27 million people visited in 2010, making it the seventh most visited country in the world.[3] Many travelers who make a friend in Turkey leave with the feeling that they have a friend for life.

Mount Ararat's highest peaks are covered with snow all year. It is seen here from Armenia, near the Turkish border. The Khor Virap monastery lies in the foreground.

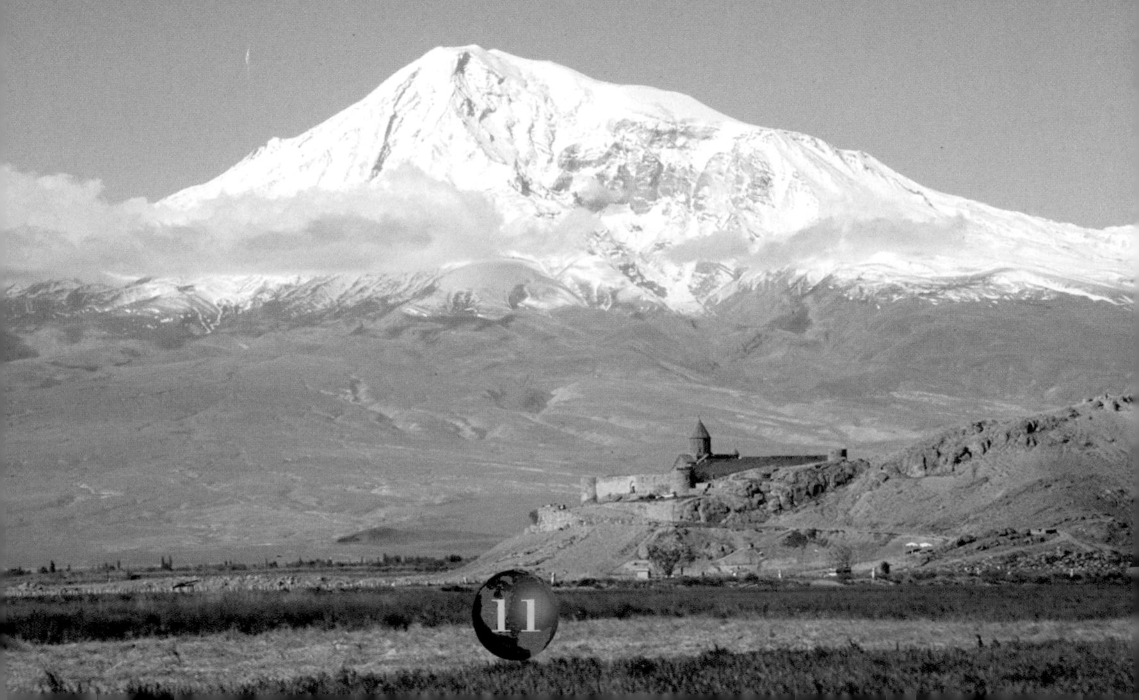

Where in the World

WHERE IN THE WORLD IS TURKEY?

1   Bosporus Strait
2   Dardanelles Strait

ISRAEL
Port Jerusalem ★ West Bank
Said
Cairo   Canal   Gaza Strip •
Dead Sea
(lowest point in Asia, -408 m)
Amman
JORDAN
Alexandria

GEORGIA
Tbilisi ★
ARMENIA
Yerevan ★
Ani
Mt Ararat
Doğubeyazit
IRAN
Van
Erzurum   E80
Trabzon
Sümela
Eastern
Anatolia
E99
Diyarbakır
Southeastern
Anatolia
E90
Mosul
Kirkuk
IRAQ
SYRIA
Aleppo
Gaziantep
Mt Nemrut
E70
Samsun
Sinop
Black Sea
Black Sea Turkey
E80
Kayseri
Cappadocia
Adana
Mersin
E90
E88
Ankara
O-4
Central
Anatolia
E90
Konya
Mediterranean
Turkey
Antalya
Mediterranean Sea
İstanbul
Bursa
Uludağ
Sea of
Marmara
Marmara
Region
E96
Pamukkale
E87
Pergamon
İzmir
Ephesus   Aegean
Turkey
Bodrum
Datça
Ölüdeniz
Aegean Sea
BULGARIA
E80
Edirne
E87
O-3
E84
Eastern Thrace
E90
E881
Troy
E87
GREECE
Gallipoli
2

150 Kilometers
150 Miles

TURKEY FACTS AT A GLANCE

Full name: Republic of Turkey

Languages: Turkish (official language), Kurdish, other minority languages

Population: 78,785,548 (July 2011 est.)

Total area: 302,535 square miles (783,562 square kilometers); slightly larger than Texas

Capital: Ankara

Government: Republican parliamentary democracy

Ethnic makeup: Turkish 70 to 75 percent, Kurdish 18 percent, other minorities 7 to 12 percent (2008 est.)

Religions: Islam 99.8 percent (mostly Sunni), other 0.2 percent (mostly Christianity and Judaism)

Exports: Clothing and textiles, fruit and vegetables, iron and steel, motor vehicles and machinery, fuels and oils

Imports: Machinery, chemicals, semi-finished goods, fuels, transport equipment

Crops: Tobacco, cotton, grain such as wheat and barley, olives, sugar beets, hazelnuts, pulses, citrus; livestock

Climate: Temperate hot, dry summers with mild, wet winters; harsher in interior

Highest point: Mount Ararat, 16,948 feet (5,166 meters)

Longest river fully contained within Turkey: Kizilirmak River, about 715 miles (1,150 kilometers) long

Flag: Turkey's flag was adopted on June 5, 1936. It features a white crescent moon and a white five-pointed star on a red background. The colors and design resemble those on the banner of the Ottoman Empire, which came before modern-day Turkey. These symbols serve as insignia for the Turks, as well as being traditional symbols of Islam. Legend says the flag represents the reflection of the moon and a star in a pool of blood spilled from Turkish warriors. It is also said that the white represents peace and honesty and the red represents bravery and strength.

National flower: Tulip (*Tulipa*)

National bird: Redwing (*Turdus iliacus*)

Sources: *BBC News:* "Turkey Country Profile," http://news.bbc.co.uk/2/hi/europe/country_profiles/1022222.stm#facts; CIA—*The World Factbook:* "Turkey"; *Flags and Nations of the World,* http://www.flags-flags-flags.org.uk/index.htm; Tina MacDonald, *Birding Hotspots Around the World:* "Turkey," http://www.camacdonald.com/birding/CountryIndex.htm#T

Ölüdeniz, which means "dead sea," is Turkey's most popular Mediterranean beach. Its stunning blue lagoon is a national nature reserve. Visitors can paraglide off nearby mountains and take in the view before landing on the beach.

Chapter 2

From Ararat to the Aegean

Turkey's place in the world has shaped its history. With the Black Sea above and the Mediterranean Sea below, Turkey is a huge bridge of land connecting Europe and Asia. This has made it a natural highway for travelers. In ancient times, Roman soldiers marched in from the west and Ottoman horsemen swept in from the east. Merchants became wealthy by traveling in both directions along the Silk Road, which started in China.

A tiny portion of Turkey—3 percent—lies in Europe and shares borders with Greece and Bulgaria. This region of fertile hills and valleys is called Eastern Thrace. The Aegean Sea separates the rest of Turkey from Greece. The inland Sea of Marmara and the Bosporus and Dardanelles straits separate Eastern Thrace from the remaining 97 percent of Turkey. Called Anatolia or Asia Minor, this part of Turkey is in Asia. Anatolia shares land borders with Georgia, Armenia, Azerbaijan, Iran, Iraq, and Syria.

Turkey is perched atop massive, shifting tectonic plates. It is one of the most earthquake-prone places in the world, and the list of deaths through the centuries is long. A 1939 quake in the dead of winter flattened the eastern city of Erzincan and caused a small tsunami that crashed onto a stretch of the Black Sea coast. At least 32,700 people were killed. In 1999, a 7.6-magnitude quake ripped through western Turkey near Izmit, toppling buildings and taking more than 17,000 lives. Half a million people were left homeless, and property damage was in the billions of dollars.[1]

Topkapi Palace in Istanbul overlooks the Golden Horn, the Bosporus Strait, and the Sea of Marmara. Built by Sultan Mehmet II in the 1470s, the palace became the heart of the Ottoman Empire. Now a museum, it houses the Topkapi Dagger, a symbol of the palace that is set with huge emeralds, and the 86-carat Kasikci Diamond.

Mountains cover most of the land—about 80 percent. The steep, rainy Pontus Mountains stretch along the northern coast, and the Taurus Mountains border the southern coast. Between them lies the high Central Anatolian Plateau. Eastern Turkey is home to the 16,948-foot (5,166-meter) Mount Ararat and Turkey's largest lake, the startlingly blue Van.

The Tigris and Euphrates rivers both spring from the mountains in southeastern Turkey. Mesopotamia, which means "land between the rivers" in ancient Greek, begins there and extends into modern Syria, Iraq, and Iran.

In 1941, a group of people called the First Geography Congress met in Turkey's capital city of Ankara. Their job was to divide the country into regions. The members considered things like climate, wildlife, agriculture, and the way people lived and moved from place to place. They divided the country into seven regions: Marmara, the Black Sea, the Mediterranean, the Aegean, Central Anatolia, Eastern Anatolia, and Southeastern Anatolia. Turkey's 81 provinces do not fit neatly into the regional plan.

Turks say you can experience all four seasons in one day if you are willing to drive far enough. That's because the weather in each region can differ so dramatically. The Mediterranean and Aegean coasts have cool winters and balmy summers. The Black Sea coast is rainy throughout the year. The Anatolian Plateau and the mountains in the east have severe, snowy winters and scorching, dry summers.

Turkey's landscape features plains, woodlands, mountains, and about 4,500 miles (7,200 kilometers) of shoreline. This diversity allows many types of plants and animals to flourish. There are more than 11,000 plant species, including its most famous, the tulip.

Turkey is a birdwatcher's paradise because it is on the flight path of dozens of species of migratory birds. In the fall, huge flocks of storks and birds of prey fly over the Bosporus. Lakes and wetlands are home to thousands of wintering waterfowl. More than 400 bird species have been sighted, including terns, partridges, and eagles.

The rugged southeast is home to large mammals, including bears, jackals, and the elusive Anatolian leopard. The mountains on both coasts are covered with trees. About a quarter of Turkey has stands of spruce, pine, and cedar.

Giant loggerhead turtles can be spotted on the beaches of southwestern Turkey, one of the few places where they still nest. People are no longer allowed on some of these beaches at night, and there are daytime restrictions on where they are allowed to plop down their towels and umbrellas.

The central plains spring into vivid life when huge swaths of yellow, blue, and pink flax and purple gladioli flower. Stinging creatures such as scorpions and snakes are found all over, and visitors to beaches and ancient ruins are warned to watch where they step.

The country is being developed rapidly, but it still has large chunks of unspoiled countryside, some of which have been made into national parks. Threats include water and air pollution, dams, deforestation, intensive farming, and people who want to take over parkland for industry.

Giant loggerhead turtle

A ten-minute scramble up a rocky slope, Karain Cave gave Paleolithic people a safe haven from enemies, dangerous animals, and bad weather. A small museum at the base of the slope contains Stone Age finds. Other artifacts are housed at the nearby Antalya Museum.

Ancient Cities and Shrines

Turkey's history is richer than gold and has more threads than a kilim carpet. Some of the world's most exciting archaeological discoveries have been made here.

People have lived in Turkey since the Stone Age. Proof lies in caves all around Anatolia, including Karain Cave in the foothills of the Taurus Mountains. Inside the cave's eerie caverns and tunnels, archaeologists have dug up skeletons of early modern humans, as well as teeth and skull fragments from a Neanderthal child. They have dug up ancient hand axes and flint hide scrapers. They have found bones from wild sheep and goats that were hurled to the cave floor after early hunters gnawed off the tasty meat and smashed open the bones to reach the rich marrow.[1] Karain was used continuously from at least 20,000 BCE up until a few hundred years ago. It was most likely visited by even earlier humans.

Anatolia has several Neolithic (New Stone Age) sites, including a remarkable one on the Konya Plain in south-central Turkey. Çatalhöyük was first settled some 9,500 years ago.[2] As many as 8,000 people lived there, side by side, making it one of the world's first cities. They grew wheat, lentils, peas, and other crops. They herded sheep and goats, and even kept dogs. Archaeologists have studied teeth that show the residents had a diet that varied over time.[3]

Çatalhöyük was occupied for well over a thousand years. It contains layer upon layer of homes, because people built new structures on top of old foundations. The mud-brick dwellings were pressed together,

GÖBEKLI TEPE: THE WORLD'S FIRST SHRINE

In southeastern Turkey on a hill overlooking a dusty plain is a place that could change our ideas about people and religion. Göbekli Tepe, "Potbelly Hill" in Turkish, contains a vast temple complex that was built by hunter-gatherers some 11,000 years ago, before the invention of writing, metal tools, or the wheel.

Archaeologists have unearthed four stone circles. Radar shows that at least sixteen are still buried across the 22-acre (9-hectare) site. The largest circle is 65 feet (20 meters) across.

About half of the fifty exposed pillars are carved with lively images of scorpions, snakes, leopards, vultures, gazelles, and other animals. Others are carved with arms and hands—their T-tops may represent faceless heads. People built the site, and then buried it, but their reasons for doing so are unclear.

Göbekli Tepe sits at the northern edge of the Fertile Crescent, home to some of the planet's earliest farmers. At a prehistoric village 20 miles (32 kilometers) away, geneticists have found evidence of the world's first domestic wheat. The age of the wheat shows that agriculture developed there about five hundred years after construction began at Göbekli Tepe.

The lead archaeologist since 1994 believes it is the first human-built holy place. Klaus Schmidt says we once thought it was only after people began farming and living in settled communities that they had the time and resources to build temples, but Göbekli Tepe tells us it was the other way around. He says the team effort to build these massive monoliths was the beginning of complex societies.[4]

and entered by holes in the roofs. Ladders descended into each house, which held a cooking hearth and a platform. People sat and slept on the platforms, and buried dead family members underneath them.

These ancient city dwellers painted murals on the plaster walls of their homes and shrines, and decorated them with animal skulls. They carved beautiful statuettes—one exciting find is a mother goddess seated on a throne decorated with lion heads. They kept their homes tidy, throwing their trash and sewage onto heaps outside of town. They used the world's first mirrors and wore beaded necklaces, copper rings, and other jewelry. They made razor-sharp tools from obsidian, a type of volcanic glass. They not only used these tools—they also traded them for things like seashells and lumber with people living hundreds of miles away.[5]

Around 2300 BCE, the Assyrians began to flourish in northern Mesopotamia. They built a network of trading colonies that stretched into central Anatolia. Their donkeys carried in cloth and tin and left

A replica of a Çatalhöyük house at the Museum of Anatolian Civilizations in Ankara

TROY: CITY OF LEGEND

One of Western literature's oldest stories is by the poet Homer, who lived in the eighth century BCE. *The Iliad* takes place during the final year of the Trojan War. Paris, a sweet-talking prince of Troy, made off with Helen, a beautiful queen from Greece. The Greeks sent a thousand ships to bring her home. Their siege lasted ten years, but they could not breach Troy's strong, high walls.

In *The Odyssey*, Homer describes how the war ended. A Greek king named Odysseus commanded his soldiers to build a huge hollow horse on wheels. Several soldiers climbed inside. Believing it was a gift from the gods, the Trojans wheeled the horse into the city. That night, as the Trojans slept, the soldiers crept out of the horse and threw open the city's gates. The rest of the Greek army flooded into Troy and attacked.

For a long time, nobody knew whether Troy was real or just the setting for an ancient tale. A German explorer named Heinrich Schliemann decided to look for Troy. Archaeologist Frank Calvert was already digging at a site in northern Turkey, at today's Hisarlik. Calvert believed he had found Troy, and Schliemann agreed to pay for the excavations.

Unfortunately, Schliemann was interested only in Homer's Troy. His crew destroyed other valuable artifacts as they dug. Schliemann also smuggled priceless objects out of Turkey. The items eventually ended up at the Pushkin Museum in Russia. Turkey still wants them back. As for Calvert, Schliemann never gave him credit for being the first to dig at Troy.

Visitors to the Troy archaeological site can climb into a replica of the Trojan horse and see the remains of the south gate where Hector and Achilles battled it out in Homer's *Iliad*. There are roadways, walls from various times in Troy's 4,000-year history, and a small amphitheater from Roman days.

with gold and silver. These merchants carefully kept track of their businesses. They wrote using cuneiform symbols they stamped onto clay tablets. Their records are the earliest examples of writing to have been discovered in Anatolia.

The Hittites

Around 2000 BCE, waves of invaders began flooding into Anatolia, probably from the Caucasus region to the northeast. They came to be known as the Hittites, and theirs was the first powerful empire to rise in Anatolia.

Over the next several centuries, the warring Hittites became experts at forging iron weapons. They used strong, fast horses to pull three-man chariots. They gained, lost, and regained territory.

The Hittite capital was at Hattusha (today's Bogâzkale). Perched on a plateau with steep ravines on three sides, it was home to wealthy nobles and warriors as well as to slaves, peasants, and talented craftsmen who specialized in pottery, carpentry, masonry, and metalwork using silver from the Taurus Mountains. The city had double walls of stone and five massive entryways, including one flanked by huge carved lions. Parts of the 20-foot- (6-meter-) high wall still stand. Replicas of the stone lions guard the gate, while the originals reside at the Museum of Anatolian Civilizations in Ankara.

The empire was at its peak by 1258 BCE when King Hattusili III signed a peace treaty with Ramses II, the pharaoh of Egypt. Several years later, Hattusili sealed the deal by sending his daughter to Egypt to marry Ramses. The Treaty of Kadesh is the earliest known recorded international peace treaty.[6] It was written on a clay tablet that was found in pieces, reassembled, and put on display at the Ancient Orient Museum in Istanbul. A copy hangs in the United Nations headquarters in New York City to remind world leaders that peace treaties are a worthy tradition.

Some 25,000 tablets with Hittite writings were found at Hattusha. The Hittites used cuneiform script, but it was not the same script the Assyrian traders used. They also used hieroglyphics on some tablets, probably so that common people could read them. Once they were deciphered in 1915, the tablets revealed their views on religion and listed their laws for free people and slaves. According to one rule, people working in the palace kitchen had to swear that the water they gave the king was pure. A single hair found floating in the royal bathwater would result in death for the person responsible.[7]

The Sea Peoples

Around 1200 BCE, warring tribes known as the Sea Peoples invaded the Mediterranean during a famine in the Hittite Empire. Many people died or fled, leaving only a shadow of the empire in southern Anatolia and northern Syria. The Assyrians stepped into the vacuum and took over many Hittite kingdoms. In the east, around Lake Van, the Urartians rose to power and ruled until the sixth century BCE.

One of the tribes of Sea Peoples destroyed Hattusha. They were probably the Phrygians, who swept in from Thrace. They eventually controlled a large part of central Anatolia, with their capital at Gordion, near today's Ankara. King Midas was the last Phrygian ruler, around the end of the eighth century BCE. He was a real man, but legend says he had the ears of a donkey and that everything he touched turned to gold.

While the Phrygians mined for gold in central Anatolia, other cultures prospered, including the Ionians, Lydians, and Lycians. The Ionians colonized the Aegean coast and had city-states at Miletus and

Lake Van is one of the world's largest lakes without an outlet—the original outlet was blocked after an ancient volcanic eruption. Van is even saltier than the sea.

Ephesus, where their philosophy, poetry, and art flourished and spread. The Lycians thrived along the Mediterranean coast. The Lydians controlled most of western Anatolia. These renowned silversmiths changed commerce with their invention of coins. The wealth of their last king, Croesus, was famed, and their capital, Sardis, near the Aegean Coast, was one of the ancient world's richest cities.

In 546 BCE, Cyrus the Great of Persia invaded and conquered most of Anatolia. For the next two centuries, the Persians ruled. Anatolia became a gateway between the East and the West along the Royal Road, a 1,600-mile (2,600-kilometer) highway the Persians built. A Greek historian named Herodotus who lived during those times described the road and its vast system of station houses that let royal messengers travel in relays across the empire at great speed. The boast above the federal post office in New York City—"Neither snow nor rain nor heat nor gloom of night stays these couriers from the swift completion of their appointed rounds"—echoes Herodotus's description of those faithful Persian messengers.[8]

Artemis of Ephesus, Museum of Ephesus

The Hellenistic Age

Alexander the Great—a young king from Macedonia (part of ancient Greece)—declared war on the Persians in the 330s BCE. His army's march against them was fierce and bloody. His victory at the Battle of Issus in 333 BCE and ultimate domination of the Persians ushered in the Hellenistic Age, which had a mixture of Greek and Asian elements. The Greek influence spread and blossomed from India to Africa, and poets and scientists alike thrived. The city of Pergamum, or Pergamon, near the Aegean coast had a library that was thought to have contained as many as 200,000 scrolls.[9]

Today, visitors can see dozens of Greek ruins throughout Turkey, including Pergamum and Ephesus, where one of the Seven Wonders of the Ancient World, the Temple of Artemis, can be found.

Whirling dervishes perform in Konya in the annual Mevlana festival. The practice of whirling started when Muslim religious men, called Sufis, believed it would help them get closer to Allah (God). The Mevlevi, the most renowned Sufi order, was founded by Mevlana Celaleddin-i Rumi in 1273. The faith was outlawed in 1925, but the government promotes the dancing as a tourist attraction.

Early Christians, Late Sultans

Some of the world's greatest empires rose and fell in Turkey, influencing customs and religions across the land. From Anatolia's high central plains to the shores of the Aegean, it's hard to imagine taking a step anywhere that hasn't already been trod upon by a statesman or a sultan, a farmer or a trader.

The Roman Age

During the second century BCE, the Romans began a fast expansion to the east. The First and Second Macedonian Wars gave them control of the entire Mediterranean basin and key cities throughout Anatolia. They built wide stone roads that made travel easier, and erected stadiums for the people's entertainment. Aqueducts brought in drinking water and filled baths and fountains. Sewers carried away waste, making cities cleaner and nicer places to live. By the second century CE, Anatolia's cities rivaled those of Rome. Meanwhile, a new religion called Christianity arose in Judea (today's Israel). Many of its important chapters would be played out in Anatolia.

The Byzantine Empire

For more than a thousand years, the Byzantines ruled over half the known world. Their two greatest emperors were Constantine and Justinian.

In 324 CE, Constantine moved to the ancient Greek colony of Byzantium and began transforming it into the New Rome. He constructed a forum and public baths, and enlarged its Hippodrome, where chariot races would thrill cheering audiences. Massive walls enclosed the city's seven hills.

The city was named Constantinople in 330 CE, and it became the capital of the Eastern Roman Empire. It would last through the Middle Ages. As Rome lost its power, Constantinople remained a sparkling jewel that stunned visitors with its wealth.

Constantine became the first Roman emperor to convert to Christianity. He presided over the bishops who met in Nicea, today's Iznik, to establish the Nicene Creed. It says that one God made heaven and earth. Anyone who opposed the creed was branded a heretic.

This was a turning point for early Christianity. Until the fourth century, there had been off-and-on persecution of Christians, whose new religion made the Romans uneasy. Now Christians were free to worship and spread their faith.

Anatolia was a cradle of Christianity. Saint Paul was born in Tarsus, Cilicia, in today's south-central Turkey. Many of his missionary journeys in the first century were to Anatolian cities. Many of Paul's and Peter's letters, called epistles, were written to believers in Anatolia. The Seven Churches of the Apocalypse in the Book of Revelation were in western Anatolia.

The Byzantines reached their peak under Emperor Justinian in the sixth century. He reclaimed vast territories that

The Green Mosque in Iznik has a single minaret. Built in the late 1300s, it was one of the first Ottoman mosques. Iznik became a capital for tile making.

had been lost in previous centuries. He rewrote Roman law, and his version is still the basis of civil law in many modern countries. One of his legacies was rebuilding the Hagia Sofia, a church that would become the center of Eastern Orthodox Christianity. The new church—with its brilliant gold dome—was opened on December 27, 537. Justinian ordered the sacrifice of 1,000 oxen, 6,000 sheep, 600 stags, and 10,000 birds, and he gave 30,000 bushels of meal to the poor.[1]

By the eleventh century, the empire was fading. Weak rulers had failed to keep up the city's defenses, and they had mismanaged its money. Its territory was shrinking under pressure from a threat to the east, the Seljuk Turks.

Constantinople remained the center of the Orthodox Christian Church, while Rome was the center of the Catholic Church. They were jealous of each other's power and influence. In 1204, Roman Catholic Crusaders sacked the Hagia Sofia, breaking holy images and hurling relics of the martyrs. The city never recovered. By the time Constantine XI inherited the imperial throne in 1449, Constantinople was a Christian enclave in the middle of the Ottoman Empire.

Emperor Justinian built the third Hagia Sofia in the sixth century CE. Mehmet II converted it to a mosque in the fifteenth century, and now it is a museum. It is sometimes called the Eighth Wonder of the Ancient World.

On May 29, 1453, a young, ambitious Ottoman sultan called Mehmet II used massive cannons to breach the walls of Constantinople. He led his fierce soldiers, the Janissaries, to the Hagia Sofia and proclaimed it as a mosque. Mehmet made Constantinople his capital, and he renamed it Istanbul.

The Seljuk Sultanate

The Seljuks were a Turkish tribe from Central Asia who invaded Persia and captured Baghdad (now in Iraq) in 1055. Their leader was crowned caliph, the ruler of the Islamic world. The Great Seljuk Sultanate was formed and would rule much of the Islamic world for the next hundred years.

The Seljuks went on to occupy Syria and Armenia, and then raided Anatolia. In 1071 they defeated the Byzantine army and took over most of Anatolia.

The victorious Seljuks formed a series of Islamic states. The best known was the Seljuk Sultanate of Rum, which established its capital at Konya around 1150. The Seljuk ruling class forged trade relations

with Byzantium and other states, and were tolerant of different races and religions. Churches and synagogues flourished alongside Seljuk architecture that included mosques, hospitals, and seminaries.

By the twelfth century, the Seljuks were under pressure from Crusaders in the west and the Mongols in the east. In 1243 the Mongols defeated the Seljuks at Kösedağ. Seljuk power was broken by 1261, and at the end of the century, chaos ruled in Anatolia.

The Ottoman Empire

In the late 1200s, the Ottomans were one of many warrior tribes galloping their sturdy horses across the Anatolian plains. Their leader was a tribal chief named Osman, whose name sounded like "Ottoman" to outsiders. The Ottomans would rule Anatolia for 600 years, and their empire would become a world force, with borders that spanned three continents.

During the early decades, the diplomatic Muslim Ottomans enlisted Christians as their allies. They promoted their best battle-hardened

The fortress of Rumeli Hisari was built in just a few months in 1452 by Sultan Mehmet II at the narrowest part of the Bosporus on the European side. From it, he cut off supplies to Constantinople before launching his attack on the city.

ISRAEL
Alexandria   Port Jerusalem   West Bank'ᴅ ᴇ ˢ ᴇ ʀ ᴛ
Said   ★Amman
CHAPTER **4** **We Visit Turkey**
Cairo   Canal Gaza Strip   Dead Sea
(lowest point in Asia, -408 m)
JORDAN

soldiers. Soon they straddled important trade routes and set up vassal states that swore allegiance to their new leaders.

One of the Ottomans' first and longest-lasting conquests was a mountainous corner of Europe where many Christians lived. They called this new territory the Balkans, which means "Forested Mountains." They traveled into Christian villages, chose the largest and strongest boys and converted them to Islam, then trained them for the military or other service to the sultan.

The empire reached its peak in the sixteenth century under Süleyman the Magnificent. His rule saw the rise of huge palaces and graceful mosques with minarets that reached to the sky. The most famous among them was Süleymaniye Mosque in Istanbul, designed by his chief architect, Sinan.

Over the next century, the empire grew until it sprawled across North Africa, Arabia, Iraq, and into Europe as far as Hungary. The Ottoman advance was halted at the gates of Vienna in 1683.

By the eighteenth century, poor leadership saw the empire stagnate and its territories wither. In 1854–1856, the Ottomans fought with Britain and France against the Russians in the Crimean Peninsula. Turkey won, but its power continued to weaken as the Europeans it had fought stirred its Balkan subjects into a rebellion.

In 1877 war broke out in the Balkans, and the insurgents were boosted to victory by Russia. The Ottomans lost most of their European possessions. In 1908 a group of reformers called the Young Turks began putting pressure on the sultan to rule in a more democratic manner. The Balkan Wars (1912–1913)—against Greece, Serbia, and Bulgaria—reduced Turkey's European territory even further. When World War I began, the Turks were on Germany's side.

Soldiers were not the only casualties of World War I. Between 1915 and 1918, more than one million Armenians were forced out of their historic homeland in eastern Turkey. Many died on long deportation marches. Other people living in Turkey, including Greek Christians, also lost their lives on these brutal marches. Civilians on both sides died of starvation and by acts of violence.

The defeat of Germany in 1918, with the resulting Treaty of Sèvres in 1920, was a low point for Turkey. The treaty gave huge swaths of

Mustafa Kemal (foreground) was a commander during the bloody Battle of Gallipoli in 1915–1916 at the Dardanelles Strait. The nine-month battle was the Ottoman Empire's final surge of resistance against the Allies in World War I. The Turks saved Constantinople, but victory came at a high cost to both sides. More than half a million soldiers were injured or killed.

territory to Great Britain and France—including Mecca and the kingdom of Hejaz. It granted autonomy to the Kurds, let Armenia become a separate republic, and gave Smyrna (today's Izmir) to the Greeks until the people living there could vote on their own fate. Greece and Italy took all of Turkey's European holdings except for Istanbul and the land around it. The Straits became international waters. Turkey was ordered to pay reparations, and the Allies clamped down on the Turkish economy. Turkey was no longer in control of its own destiny.

By now the Young Turks were fighting for their country's independence from their base in Ankara. They were led by a man named Mustafa Kemal, who would later take the name Atatürk.

The War for Independence
In 1919, Greece began sending soldiers into Smyrna, to hold on to its share of Turkish land. The Young Turks and their troops fought back. In 1920, they formed the Turkish Grand National Assembly. Their fight became the nation's fight.

By 1922, Turkey had won its War of Independence. On October 29, 1923, a secular nationalist republic was declared, and Mustafa Kemal was unanimously elected the first president of the Republic of Turkey.

MUSTAFA KEMAL ATATÜRK: FATHER OF THE TURKS

Mustafa Kemal Atatürk's bold vision and firm rule led to deep and lightning-fast changes for the country. "Kemalism"—as his ideas came to be known—centered on freedom and equality for all citizens. "We are a nation without classes or special privileges," Atatürk said.

He served as president for fifteen years until his death from liver disease. He eliminated the sultanate and established the separation of government and religion.

Under Atatürk, women were given the right to vote, and girls were sent to school. He modernized the classical village education. Polygamy was abolished. Western clothes were introduced, and the veil for women and fez for men were outlawed.

In 1926 the first penal code, based on the Swiss model, was established and the Islamic courts were closed. Arabic words were purged from the language, and the Arabic script was replaced with a Latin one in a matter of months. Atatürk himself traveled the country, teaching people the new alphabet. An international number system was introduced. A Western calendar replaced the Islamic one. All citizens took surnames—until then, people had a first name and then took their father's name. Mustafa Kemal was given his new surname by the people. *Atatürk* means "father of the Turks."

He died at the age of 57 in his bedroom at Dolmabahçe Palace in Istanbul on November 10, 1938. Out of respect, the clock in his room is stopped at the exact time: 9:05 A.M. His remains were brought to Ankara, where they lie in Anıtkabir ("monumental tomb"). The stern pillared building rises from grand stairs set at the end of a sweeping plaza. Millions of people visit every year.

Mustafa Kemal Atatürk

Dolmabahçe Palace, Istanbul

Atatürk's image can be found all across Turkey. There are statues of him in practically every town square, including at Gallipoli. His photograph hangs in public offices, schools, and stores. Many facilities are named after him, such as the Atatürk Bridge over the Golden Horn, the Atatürk International Aiport in Istanbul, and the impressive Atatürk Dam on the Euphrates River. Every year on November 10, at 9:05 A.M., traffic stops and people pause for one minute in remembrance.

Atatürk is still so widely respected in Turkey that it is illegal to criticize him. Movies and books that show his human side—saying, for instance, that his final years were lonely— are hotly debated. The state-owned Internet provider was forced by a court order to block YouTube in 2007 after videos making fun of Atatürk were posted.

Dolmabahçe
Clock Tower, Istanbul

Abdullah Gül, Turkey's eleventh president, was born on October 29, 1950. A member of the Justice and Development Party (AKP), his presidency began in 2007. He was Turkey's Minister of Foreign Affairs from 2003 to 2007; before that he served a four-month stint as prime minister.

How Turkey Runs

Turkey is one of the few Muslim nations to have a democracy. Its constitution guarantees equal rights for everyone, regardless of race, gender, or religion. Its laws are based on the Swiss Civil Code, not on *sharia,* or Islamic law.

The Turkish government is a parliamentary republic that uses a constitution as its roadmap for running the country. Its legislature, executive branch, and judiciary are independent of one another. In its executive branch are a president and a prime minister. The president is the head of state and makes sure the constitution is followed. He or she can veto laws that are passed by the parliament. The prime minister leads the Council of Ministers. In 2011 there were twenty-five ministers, each in charge of one area (such as finance, tourism, health care, or agriculture). One oversaw Turkey's bid to join the European Union.[1]

The parliament, called the Grand National Assembly, has 550 elected members who each serves a term of four years, although general elections may be called at any time. Several parties may battle it out during the election. A party must get at least 10 percent of the country's votes in order to win seats in parliament. The seats are divided among the parties, according to the percentage of votes they receive. The president appoints the prime minister—traditionally the leader of the party with the most seats.

President Abdullah Gül was elected to a seven-year term by the parliament in 2007. That same year, Turkey's people voted to change

A Turk casts his vote into a clear ballot box in Izmir during the 2011 parliamentary election.

the constitution. It called for the next president to be elected to a five-year term by the people instead of by the parliament. There is a two-term limit.

Turks take their right to vote very seriously. There are about 50 million registered voters, who must be 18 or older. An incredible 87 percent of them turned out for the June 2011 parliamentary elections.[2] Polling places don't have to be wheelchair accessible, but that does not stop determined Turks from casting their ballots, even if friends or relatives have to carry them up three flights of stairs.

Voters mark paper ballots. At the 2011 parliamentary election, they dropped them into new, clear boxes designed to prevent cheating.

Elections in Turkey are exciting. Several parties vie for power in the country's 81 voting districts. In the weeks leading up to polling day, colorful banners with catchy slogans are hung everywhere. Headlines scream the latest details about the hotly contested race.

Turkey has a history of banning political parties, too, with members resurfacing in new parties. That was the case with the founders of Turkey's ruling Justice and Development Party (AKP). They once belonged to the Welfare Party (RP), which waas shut down in 1998 for not respecting Turkey's secular principles.[3]

The AKP, headed by Prime Minister Recep Tayyip Erdoğan, swept to its third consecutive victory with its greatest share of the vote to that point, almost 50 percent. That gave it 326 seats in the Grand National Assembly. Other parties gaining enough votes to enter parliament included the opposition Republican People's Party, the Nationalist Action Party, and the pro-Kurdish Peace and Democracy Party. Women were given 78 seats, a new record.

Turkey's military has long considered itself to be the guardian of the country's secular constitution. Since 1960, it has toppled three governments whose Islamist leanings were considered a threat. The AKP has fought back. In 2010, it jailed dozens of military officers and accused them of taking part in a plot called Sledgehammer to stir up political chaos that would justify another military takeover.

One of the AKP's campaign promises was to revamp Turkey's 1982 constitution, which was written by military officers who had taken

Turkey's Prime Minister Recep Tayyip Erdoğan waves to a crowd of supporters at a June 2011 rally. Erdoğan's ambitions include what he calls his "crazy" plans to build a canal from the Black Sea to the Marmara Sea and a third bridge over the Bosporus Strait. He hoped to accomplish these and other economic improvements by the year 2023.

over the government two years earlier. A new constitution may help Turkey in its quest to qualify for membership in the European Union, a top priority for the nation. Negotiations for its entry began in October 2005. In order to qualify, Turkey was told to meet a long list of conditions called the Copenhagen criteria. The conditions address a range of issues, from Turkey's stance on human rights to how it treats its Kurdish minority and its dealings with Cyprus. Turkey has been working to meet the criteria, but observers say it will be a long process.

On the local level, a governor is appointed to each of the country's 81 provinces. The provinces are divided into municipalities and villages. Police monitor the cities and towns, and Turkey's military police are in charge of rural areas.

Turkey's judiciary enforces the laws. Civilian and military courts are separate. Turkey's courtrooms do not have juries—verdicts are handed down by a judge or a panel of three judges.

A Booming Economy

When Atatürk began Turkey's modernization, most people lived in the sleepy countryside, and the main industry was agriculture. Today Turkey's booming population is centered in its cities.

Europe is still its biggest market, and Turkey values its ties with the West. However, its location—and its "zero problems with its neighbors" policy—has seen Turkey opening markets in the Middle East, Russia, and China. Turkey exports building materials, food, clothes, car parts, and consumer electronics, among others. Turkish construction, shipbuilding, and engineering companies also thrived during the boom.

The country drew up action plans for 2023, which marks the hundredth anniversary of the Turkish Republic. They include becoming one of the world's top ten economies, a top-five tourist destination, and home to one of the tenth-largest ports. It also plans to be using 20 percent less energy, and have three nuclear power plants up and running.

The rapid pace of development and population growth requires increased energy production. A massive public works plan will put dams for hydro-electric power on many of Turkey's rivers. Critics worry

At a Bozkurt textile factory in Kahramanmaraş, workers make clothing, which is one of the largest exports of Turkey.

that the dams will damage Turkey's delicate ecological balance, create deserts out of fields, drive farmers off their land, and destroy forests and other dwindling natural habitats.[4]

Turkey reordered its currency, so now you don't have to be a millionaire to go to the movies or buy an ice cream cone. In 2005, it dropped six zeroes from the Turkish lira and created currency called the New Turkish Lira. With the change, a one million-lira note became a one-lira note. The "new" was dropped in January 2009 when Turkey's Central Bank issued redesigned bills and coins with features that made them harder to counterfeit.

Turkey's coins are called kurus. One lira has one hundred kurus. The coins come in denominations of five, ten, twenty-five, and fifty kurus. There is also a one-lira coin. Atatürk is pictured on all of Turkey's money.

A man peddles glasses of tea. Black tea, one of Turkey's favorite drinks, is made so strong that most people drink it out of small, tulip-shaped glasses. Some of the world's tastiest tea is grown in the damp Black Sea region.

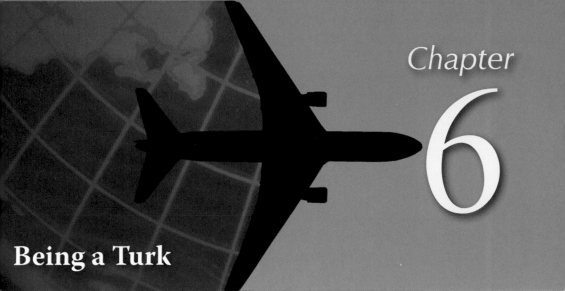

Being a Turk

Modern Turkey is a vibrant nation on the cusp of change. Its people embrace new ways while holding on to the old. More than 35 million people regularly log on to the Internet.[1] Some of those same people read coffee grounds to determine the future or wear blue-and-white beads to protect against the evil eye.

Turkey has a young population, and more than 70 percent of its people live in fast-growing urban centers. Hundreds of Turks flood out of rural areas and into its cities every week, but they still value the concept of hometown, *memleket,* and are loyal toward people from the same area.

Turkey still has thousands of villages scattered around the country where lifestyles remain mostly traditional. Women go into the fields to pick cotton and men herd sheep that have bells around their necks— but many people return to homes that have a satellite dish on the roof.

As in many countries around the world, family values are shifting as young people use the Internet and advise their parents on which cell phones and laptops to buy. Despite that, respect for the elderly and for superiors in the workplace and society plays a central role in their lives. It is not uncommon to see a young person stand up when someone older or more socially prominent enters a room.

Turkey's young people still observe the traditional division between men and women, too. Only half of them have friends of both genders, according to a poll by the Turkish government.[2] Some of those kids might not mind having friends of the opposite sex, but they are too shy or their parents won't allow it. Still, nearly a quarter of teenagers do not approve of opposite-gender friendships.

Religion

About 99 percent of Turks are Muslim, although not all of them actively practice this religion. In mosques all over Turkey, from the smallest towns to the largest cities, a muezzin cries out five times a day to let people know it is time to stop what they are doing, face Mecca, and pray. The muezzin used to climb stairs to the top of a minaret so that his melodic chant could be heard far and wide, but today most muezzins use a recording and loudspeakers.

Strict Muslims do not eat pork or drink alcohol. They follow the five pillars of Islam: They recite the creed, "There is no god but Allah and Muhammad is his prophet." They fast during the month of Ramadan (some people are exempt from this, including young children, travelers, and pregnant women). They give to the poor. If possible they make at least one pilgrimage to Mecca, called the *Hajj,* in their lifetime.

The Koran is Islam's holy book. Muslims believe it is the word of God as revealed to the prophet Muhammad.

Before entering a mosque, worshipers perform their ablutions at faucets outside. They take off their shoes and socks and wash their feet, hands, and faces. Women cover their hair and necks and wear modest clothing.

Most of Turkey's Muslims follow the Sunni branch of Islam. *Sunni* means "well-trodden path." Sunnis are very tolerant of diverse opinions as long as people recognize the basic beliefs of the faith. About a quarter of Muslims are Sufis or Alevis.

Turkey generally allows freedom of religion, and most of the one percent who are not Muslim practice Christianity or Judaism.

Clothes

Turks enjoy wearing designer clothes and showing off their fashion sense. Their cities and malls are filled with boutiques offering the latest styles. Even modest Muslim women express their fashion sense with

Prayers are offered inside the Blue Mosque, whose six minarets dominate the Istanbul skyline.

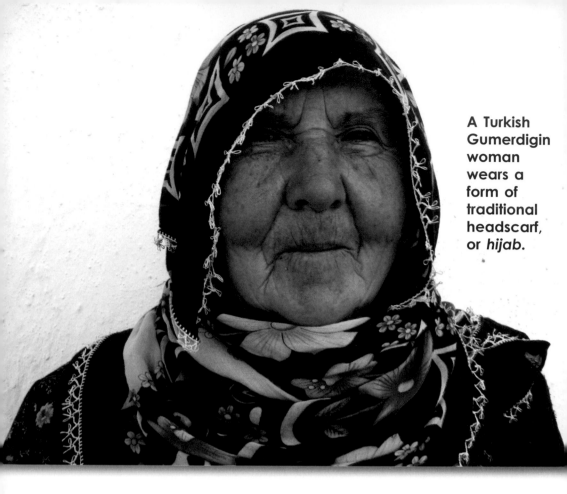

A Turkish Gumerdigin woman wears a form of traditional headscarf, or *hijab*.

the *hijab,* the religious headscarf. They choose elegant fabrics like silk in rich colors and patterns, and tie them elaborately at the neck.

Like so many other things in Turkey, the *hijab* is a symbol for a bigger issue—freedom of religious expression. The garment was banned in 1997 at Turkish universities, causing thousands of women to stay away or go abroad to study.[3] The more Islamist-leaning government elected by the people in 2002 sought to soften this rule—the AKP's prime minister and president are married to women who opt to wear the *hijab.* Since the AK party came to power, a growing number of people say they think of themselves as Muslim first and Turkish second.

Many observant Turkish Muslim women (perhaps 30 percent of the female population) dress in a *tesettür,* a headscarf and light cover-all topcoat, when going out in public. This satisfies the Islamic admonition to modest dress without infringing Turkish law, which prohibits religious dress in public places.

Education

School is mandatory for Turkish kids, starting at the age of six. They must attend for at least eight years. Public schools have crowded classrooms with as many as fifty students per teacher. Private schools offer smaller class sizes. All Turkish public school students must wear uniforms.

Elementary school children start the day with a pledge of allegiance. It opens with the lines: "I am a Turk, I am honest and I am a hard worker. My duty is to protect those younger than me and respect my elders." It also praises Atatürk's vision for Turkey.

High school students in Turkey attend standard public schools, as well as science high schools, vocational schools, and Anatolian high schools that compete with expensive private schools by offering classes in English, German, and French.

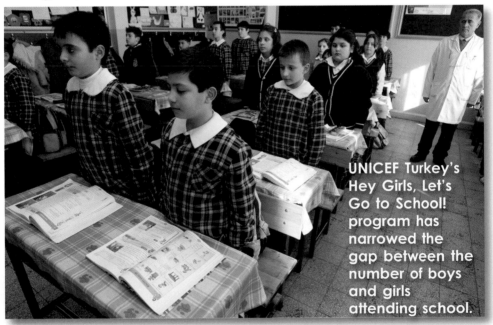

UNICEF Turkey's Hey Girls, Let's Go to School! program has narrowed the gap between the number of boys and girls attending school.

There are more than fifty universities in Turkey, and to get in, students must take a two-part examination. Many teens spend a year studying at a private school (*ozel dershaneler*) in order to pass this difficult test.

After university, military service is mandatory for men. They must serve for fifteen months—less if they are a university graduate.

Some of Turkey's favorite traditional foods include *sarma* (stuffed grape leaves), dolmas, baklava, *gözleme*, pilaf, and *börek*.

Turkey at the Table

Life in Turkey cannot be separated from its delicious food. Meals are a time when the entire family happily gathers. "It is unthinkable that . . . teenage children should eat at a separate time of their own choosing and equally unlikely that a mother should make her often tiring work outside the home a reason for failing to prepare a meal," says Turkish food expert Ayla Algar.[1]

Hospitality is a treasured Turkish trait, and unexpected guests are greeted with real pleasure. They are not only plied with delicious food, but they are often sent home carrying leftovers.

Writer Berrin Torolsan remembers how his grandmother made *puf börek,* tiny pies stuffed with melted cheese and eggs, seasoned with parsley and dill, and deep-fried; the insides melted and the outer pastry shell became crispy, crunchy, and golden. His grandmother sometimes stacked the *börek* so high he couldn't see the person sitting across the table from him. His family members moaned when she brought out plate after plate, wondering aloud who was going to eat all that food. But there never seemed to be leftovers, he recalls.[2]

Sometimes people fill their *börek* with minced, spicy meat, and other times they use spinach. When nuts and honey are stuffed into layers and layers of flaky pastry flattened so thin you can almost see through it, the result is a mouthwatering dessert called baklava.

The pastry is made from bread called *yufka,* which is sold in city market stalls and villages all over Turkey. It is a thin sheet of dough that is rolled into a huge, flat circle and cooked on an iron griddle.

The bread is unleavened, meaning no yeast is added to make it rise, so it stays flat and lasts a long time. Most cooks use modern ovens now, but some women—especially rural villagers—go to the trouble of building and then stoking a fire outdoors. They make several sheets at a time. When they're done, they have a high stack of two-foot- (60-centimeter-) wide *yufkas*.

Another popular food that has been served in Turkey for as long as anyone can remember is dolmas, or "stuffed things." The stuffing is often ground meat, such as lamb, and the wrapping is soft cabbage or grape leaves.

Food is woven into the Turkish calendar, with special dishes served during religious holidays and rites of passage. In days gone by, when two families agreed that their son and daughter would marry, everyone enjoyed *lokum,* or Turkish delight. It was hoped that the sweetness from this chewy, rosewater-flavored candy would somehow seep into the marriage.[3] At the circumcision of a male child—an important rite of passage that takes place when he is four or five years old—celebrants dine on dishes like delicious pilaf, which is rice cooked in a seasoned broth. Anything can be added to pilaf, from meat to vegetables. Guests might also be plied with *helva,* a dense sugary wheat confection.

Ramadan is a month of dawn-to-dusk fasting for the Muslims who make up most of the population. The meals served after the sun sinks below the horizon are prepared with loving care, and the day's hunger pangs make the food taste even better. *Iftar,* which means "breaking the fast," used to be announced with a cannon blast or a shot fired from a mosque. Today most people mark the time with their television, where a ticker tape at the bottom of the screen shows the exact time of *iftar* for each town.

Iftar begins with something light, like a plump date or a small bowl of olives, followed by the sunset prayer. Then comes a delicious feast where

Lokum

women serve their best recipes, including *pide* (bread), hot soups, kebabs, salads, vegetables, and eggs cooked with *pastırma.* This air-cured, pressed meat may have begun with Turkish horsemen who tucked meat into their saddles, where it was pressed flat by their legs as they rode. Meat from lambs, goats, and even camels was once used to make *pastırma,* but today beef is the chosen meat. Ramadan is a time to feed the less fortunate, and tents are erected in the town center to provide free *iftar* meals.

Another important festival on the Islamic calendar is Kirban Bayramı, the Feast of Sacrifice. It commemorates the Koranic story that tells how Abraham was ready to sacrifice his son Ishmael to Allah. On the first day of this four-day holiday, an animal is slaughtered and the meat is given to the poor. In Turkey the sacrificial animal is usually a sheep, and as the festival draws near, the unwary animals can be seen tied to trees in surprising settings, like on busy city blocks.[4] The meat is roasted in a dish called *kavurma. Helva* prepared with fat from the slaughtered animal is a traditional dessert.

The Turks love their sweets, including *tavuk göğsü.* This creamy, smooth milk pudding is made using an unlikely ingredient: a just-killed chicken. The white breast meat is boiled and the meat fibers are separated into the finest of threads. Then it's mixed with milk, sugar, cracked rice, and a flavoring like cinnamon. It is sometimes served with a dark-brown, almost burned, top.

Dessert becomes performance art with *maraş dondurması,* a type of Turkish ice cream so thick it can be eaten with a knife and fork. Street vendors love to tease their customers by presenting a scoop of the sticky ice cream and then pulling it back at the last minute, leaving the customer holding an empty cone.

Turkish coffee may be famous in the rest of the world, but tea, *çay,* is what most Turks drink. They brew it in samovars, and they like it hot, strong, and served with cubes of sugar, but not milk or lemon. The tea is grown in Turkey's Black Sea region, where mountains guard the narrow coastline. Every flat place, and even the slopes that aren't too steep, is farmed. This is also the region where most of the world's hazelnuts are grown. The bees that visit these trees make fragant honey used in the sweets that Turkish people love so well.

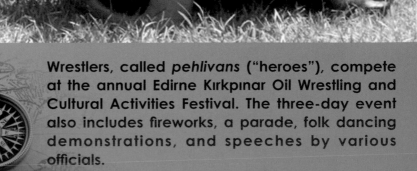

Wrestlers, called *pehlivans* ("heroes"), compete at the annual Edirne Kırkpınar Oil Wrestling and Cultural Activities Festival. The three-day event also includes fireworks, a parade, folk dancing demonstrations, and speeches by various officials.

Turks at Play

Grease wrestling, or *yagli güres,* is Turkey's national sport. Matches take place all over the country throughout the year, but the biggest event is the three-day-long contest at Kırkpınar near Edirne in Eastern Thrace. It is held in late June or early July, and as many as a thousand wrestlers compete under the brutally hot sun for the title of *baspehlivan* (chief wrestler). Turkey's president or prime minister traditionally presents the champion with the golden belt on the final day.

Wrestlers wear nothing but leather shorts called *kisbet,* which were traditionally made from the skin of a water buffalo, but are now made of cowhide or canvas. The *kisbet* are laced tightly at the knees to keep an opponent from getting a good grip. Wrestlers slather themselves in olive oil—during the Kırkpınar tournament, more than two tons of oil are used.[1]

Before a time limit was put in place, bouts could last for hours or even days, but in 1975 a limit of 30 to 40 minutes was set. Each bout features a lot of intense staring and short bursts of mighty fury. A win comes when one wrestler lifts his opponent up and takes three paces or forces the other man onto his back.

The annual tournament has been held every year since 1362, making it one of the world's longest-running sporting competitions. During the Ottoman Empire, wrestlers went to a special school to learn the art. They oiled one another to show respect. If a younger wrestler beat an older wrestler, he kissed his hand, also as a sign of respect. Today, boys learn the sport as early as the age of seven and aim to progress through its five levels.

Another type of wrestling that is popular in western Turkey takes place between camels. Thousands of people gather every winter in Selçuk and other towns on the Aegean coast to watch these bouts, which feature drooling males decked out in colorful blankets and saddles adorned with jangling bells. Their handlers hold ropes attached to tight halters that keep them from biting each other.

Most of the large wrestling camels, called *tülü,* come from Iran or Afghanistan, where they are bred for the Turkish market. The camels fight over females, and sometimes a female is paraded before the males to get them worked up. A win is declared when a camel is forced to the ground or it flees—sometimes into the crowd. Announcers use a loudspeaker to comment on the match, and those attending can buy snacks, including camel sausage.

The sport has been around since ancient times, in the days when camels were essential to the lives of nomads. In the early years of the modern Turkish republic (the 1920s), the sport was frowned on because it seemed backward, but in the 1980s it was revived as a tourist attraction and a way for people to remember their roots. By 2011, there were some 2,000 camel owners, most of them with money to burn on these beasts, which could cost up to $30,000 each.[2]

Camel wrestling

One of the most popular sports in Turkey is soccer, which Turks call football. Turkey has men's and women's national football teams, but most Turks also root for one of the nation's "big three": Galatasaray, Fenerbahçe, and Beşiktaş.

Other mainstream sports are popular, including basketball, volleyball, weightlifting, and racing—in cars and boats. The Turkish Grand Prix is a Formula One auto race that was first held in August 2005 at Istanbul Park. The 3.3-mile- (5.3 kilometer-) long track goes counterclockwise and has fourteen corners, including Turn 8, which has been nicknamed Diabolica and is one of the trickiest in Formula One racing. Formula One Group CEO Bernie Ecclestone has called it "the best racetrack in the world."[3]

Paragliding, snorkeling, surfing, and snowboarding are also popular, and Turkey offers fantastic venues for these sports.

For those who prefer hikes to headlong runs down snowy slopes, Turkey offers some of the most beautiful trails in the world. They include the 316-mile (509-kilometer) Lycian Way, which stretches along Turkey's Mediterranean coast and offers views of the sunken ruins at Üçagiz. Another is the path up Nemrut Mountain to the mausoleum of Antiochus I, which features enormous stone heads that hikers can stroll around. It is one of the nine UNESCO World Heritage Sites in Turkey where people can touch history.

For those who aren't sporty, there is still plenty to do—even if it's just reading a newspaper article about progress on the tunnel that will let trains speed under the Bosporus or a novel by Orhan Pamuk, the first Turk to win a Nobel Prize. From the jewel of Istanbul, the only city in the world to straddle two continents, to the majestic Mount Ararat, Turkey has something for everyone.

Red Bull Racing Team

Turkish Revani

Revani is a sweet sponge cake said to be named after a sixteenth-century Ottoman poet named Revani, who wrote about glorious banquets. Have **an adult** help you with the stove and oven.

Cake Ingredients
4 eggs
½ cup sugar
zest of 1 lemon
1 Tbs olive oil
½ cup semolina (farina)
⅓ cup flour
1 Tbs baking powder

Syrup Ingredients
2 cups sugar (more or less to taste)
2½ cups water
½ lemon, juiced
Optional: ¼ cup crushed nuts
       (pistachios, almonds, or walnuts
       are all delicious in revani)

Directions
1. Separate egg whites from egg yolks.
2. Beat together yolks, sugar, lemon zest, and olive oil until creamy.
3. In a separate bowl, combine semolina, flour, and baking powder.
4. Add semolina mix to egg yolk mixture and beat well. (It will be very dry.)
5. Beat egg whites with a pinch of salt to make stiff peaks. Use a wooden spoon to fold egg whites into the egg yolk mixture until creamy.
6. Pour mixture into greased 9-inch-square cake pan or Pyrex dish. Bake at 300°F for 45 minutes or until golden brown.
7. While the cake bakes, combine sugar, water, and lemon juice in a small pot. Boil the mixture, stirring well, until the sugar dissolves. Let it simmer for 10 minutes.
8. Remove the cake from the oven and cut it into 3-inch squares.
9. Pour the syrup over the servings of cake and, if you'd like, sprinkle each one with nuts. Allow the cake to cool before serving.
10. Store any leftovers in the refrigerator.

Turkish Iznik Tiles

Iznik in western Anatolia was once a center for making ceramic tiles. At first, the artists imitated the Chinese porcelain so prized by Ottoman sultans; but by the late sixteenth century, they had come into their own. Their beautiful and unique work can still be seen decorating mosques, palaces, and museums around Turkey.

You can make paper versions of Iznik tiles. Use the Internet to find examples of them, then use your creativity to make your own. You can make two, three, four, or more tiles at a time. When they are hung together, it looks nice if the tiles are all the same size and have similar patterns—but you don't have to do it that way.

You will need
Several sheets of construction paper in various colors
Ruler
Pencil
Scissors
Glue stick

Instructions
1. Choose a color for your background tiles—white is a good choice because it will make your patterns pop. You'll want to make the tiles square, so use a ruler to measure then mark your cutting lines. Put all of your background paper in a stack and cut them out at one time.
2. Fold another color of construction paper several times to make layers. Draw a simple pattern on the top layer. Hold the paper tightly and cut out the pattern, making sure to cut all the layers at once.
3. Repeat this process with different colored papers and shapes. Simple, strong shapes will give your tiles a bold look. As you become more confident, you can make smaller, more complicated shapes.
4. Arrange your cutouts on your tiles. You can make them all identical, or you can vary them slightly, depending on your mood. When you like what you see, use the glue stick to glue them in place.

ISRAEL
Alexandria
Port Jerusalem
Said
Amman
West Bank D E S E R T
TIMELINE
Cairo
Suez
Canal
Gaza Strip
Dead Sea
(lowest point in Asia, −408 m)
JORDAN

BCE	(These dates are approximate.)
20,000	Hunter-gatherers use Karain Cave on Turkey's Mediterranean coast.
9000	Construction begins at Göbekli Tepe, which is perhaps the world's first holy place.
7500	Çatalhöyük is settled; by about 6800 BCE, it has thousands of residents.
2300	Assyrian trading colonies begin to sprout up around Anatolia.
1258	The Hittite Empire reaches its peak, and King Hattusili III signs a peace treaty with Egypt.
1200	Tribes known as the Sea Peoples invade the Mediterranean.
1190	The Trojan War is fought between Greece and Troy, possibly in what is now Hisarlik, Turkey.
1000	The Urartians rise to power in the region of Lake Van.
800	The Phrygians rise to power in central and southeastern Anatolia.
700	The remaining Hittite kingdoms are taken over by Assyria.
546	Cyrus the Great of Persia conquers Sardis, the capital of the Lydian Empire.
334	Alexander the Great marches into Anatolia and within a year wins a major battle against the Persians at Issus.
196	After the Romans fight the First and Second Macedonian wars (214 to 205 and 200 to 196), they gain control of Anatolia.
CE	
1	Saint Paul (Saul of Tarsus) is born in Cilicia. He will establish the first churches in Anatolia.
312	Constantine, the Eastern Roman emperor, converts to Christianity.
330	Constantinople becomes the capital of the Eastern Roman Empire.
527	Justinian becomes the emperor of the Eastern Roman Empire.
1018	The Seljuk Turks invade Anatolia, then go on to defeat the Byzantines at the Battle of Manzikert in 1071.
1071	The Seljuk Sultanate of Rum rules, eventually building its capital in Konya.
1204	Roman Catholic Crusaders sack the Hagia Sofia.
1243	Mongol forces defeat the Seljuk army at Kösedağh.
1273	Mystic poet Rumi inspires the Whirling Dervish Sufi order.
1299	Osman sets up principalities in the western part of the Seljuk lands. He is the first Ottoman ruler to call himself sultan.
1453	Constantinople falls to Sultan Mehmet II and is renamed Istanbul.
1566	The Ottoman Empire reaches its peak under Sultan Süleyman the Magnificent.
1699	The Treaty of Karlowitz marks the beginning of the Ottoman Empire's decline as it starts to lose European territory.
1854–1856	The Ottoman Empire fights alongside France and Britain against the Russians in the Crimean War.
1912–1913	The Ottoman Empire loses most of its European possessions during the Balkan Wars.
1914	The Ottoman Empire enters World War I on Germany's side. Allied troops invade Gallipoli and are defeated by Ottoman forces led by Mustafa Kemal. Germany and its allies are defeated in 1918.
1919	The Turkish resistance begins the War of Independence from its base in Ankara.
1920	The Treaty of Sèvres gives large swaths of Turkey and control over its economy to the Allies. The treaty is signed by representatives of the sultan but is not recognized by the newly formed Grand National Assembly based in Ankara.
1922	The Turks win their War of Independence, and the Grand National Assembly abolishes the sultanate.
1923	On October 29, the Republic of Turkey is declared, and Mustafa Kemal is elected its first president. He later takes the last name of Atatürk.
1938	On November 10, Atatürk dies at 9:05 A.M. at the age of 57.

1945	On February 23, after remaining neutral for most of World War II, Turkey enters on the side of the Allies, mostly as a ceremonial gesture, and becomes a charter member of the United Nations.
1952	Turkey joins NATO, the North Atlantic Treaty Organization.
1974	Turkey invades the Republic of Cyprus after a Greek military coup on the island. It forms the Turkish Republic of Northern Cyprus, which is not recognized by the European Union or the United Nations. The Kurdistan Workers Party (PKK) fights for rights for Kurdish people living in Turkey and to establish an independent Kurdish state. The PKK is listed as a terrorist organization by the U.S., one of Turkey's NATO allies.
1982	Turkey adopts a new constitution.
2005	Turkey applies for entry to the European Union. It reorders its currency.
2006	Orhan Pamuk is awarded the Nobel Prize in Literature.
2010	The AKP jails military officers implicated in the Sledgehammer plot.
2011	The Justice and Development Party (AKP) sweeps to its third victory in the country's parliamentary elections after two previous terms that saw it strengthening the country's economy.

CHAPTER NOTES

Introduction
1. Clayton R. Koppes, "Captain Mahan, General Gordon, and the Origins of the Term 'Middle East,' " *Middle Eastern Studies*, Vol. 12, No. 1, January 1976.

Chapter 1. A Rich Blend
1. CIA—*The World Factbook*, "Turkey," https://www.cia.gov/library/ publications/the-world-factbook/ geos/tu.html
2. Rory MacLean, *Magic Bus: On the Hippie Trail from Istanbul to India* (New York: Ig Publishing, 2009), p. 64.
3. *UNWTO World Tourism Highlights*, Edition 2011, p. 6, http://www.unwto.org/facts/menu.html

Chapter 2. From Ararat to the Aegean
1. United States Geological Survey: "Historic World Earthquakes," http://earthquake.usgs.gov/ earthquakes/world/historical_country. php#turkey

Chapter 3. Ancient Cities and Shrines
1. Levent Atici, "Implications of Age Structures for Epipaleolithic Hunting Strategies in the Western Taurus Mountains, Southwest Turkey," *Anthropozoologica*, 2009, p. 22.

2. Michael Balter, *The Goddess and the Bull, Çatalhöyük: An Archaeological Journey to the Dawn of Civilization* (New York: Free Press. 2005), p. 335.
3. Ibid., pp. 154–155.
4. Andrew Curry, "Göbekli Tepe: The World's First Temple?" *Smithsonian*, November 2008.
5. William Carl Eichman, "Catal Huyuk: The Temple City of Prehistoric Anatolia," *Gnosis*, Spring 1990, http://www.telesterion.com/catal1.htm.
6. Bernard McDonagh, *Blue Guide Turkey, The Aegean and Mediterranean Coasts* (New York: W W Norton & Company, 1989), p. 24.
7. Ibid., p. 25.
8. James Romm, *Herodotus* (New Haven, Conn.: Yale University. 1998), pp. 45–46.
9. Craig Koester, *Cities of Revelation*, "Pergamum: Library," http://www2.luthersem.edu/ckoester/ Revelation/Pergamum/Library.htm

Chapter 4. Early Christians, Late Sultans
1. Lord Kinross and the Editors of the Newsweek Book Division, *Hagia Sophia* (New York: Newsweek, 1972), p. 15.

Chapter 5. How Turkey Runs

1. Associated Press, "Turkey Merges Some Ministries, Creates New Ones Ahead of Elections," *The Canadian Press,* June 8, 2011, http://ca.news.yahoo.com/turkey-merges-ministries-creates-ones-ahead-elections-111955588.html
2. "Turkey's Election: AK All Over Again," *The Economist,* June 16, 2011, http://www.economist.com/node/18836458?story_id=18836458&CFID=166236394&CFTOKEN=86903163
3. Chris Morris, "Turkey Bans Islamist Party," *The Guardian,* January 17, 1998, http://www.guardian.co.uk/world/1998/jan/17/turkey
4. Fiachra Gibbons and Lucas Moore, "Turkey's Great Leap Forward Risks Cultural and Environmental Bankruptcy," *The Guardian,* May 29, 2011, http://www.guardian.co.uk/world/2011/may/29/turkey-nuclear-hydro-power-development

Chapter 6. Being a Turk

1. Internet World Stats, "Internet Users in Europe: Usage and Population Statistics," March 31, 2011, http://www.internetworldstats.com/stats4.htm
2. "Majority of Turkish Youth Against Premarital Sex," *Hurriyet Daily News,* February 14, 2011, http://www.hurriyetdailynews.com/n.php?n=majority-of-turkish-youth-against-sex-before-wedlock-2011-02-14
3. "Turkey Eases Ban on Headscarves," *BBC News,* February 9, 2008, http://news.bbc.co.uk/2/hi/europe/7236128.stm

Chapter 7. Turkey at the Table

1. Barrie Kerper (editor), *Istanbul: The Collected Traveler* (New York: Vintage Departures, 2009), p. 311.
2. Ibid., p. 346.
3. Ibid., p. 316.
4. Ibid., p. 315.

Chapter 8. Turks at Play

1. Cindy van Vliet, "Yagli Güres: Slippery, Muscular Gladiators," *Hello Alanya Magazine,* 2010, http://www.hello-alanya.com/index.php?option=com_content&view=article&id=128%3Ayagli-gures&catid=47%3Aculture&Itemid=65
2. Joe Parkinson, "What's a Bigger Draw Than a Camel Fight? A Camel Beauty Contest, of Course." *The Wall Street Journal,* January 22, 2011, http://online.wsj.com/article/SB10001424052748704678004576089830885948812.html
3. BBC Sport, "Turkey to Keep F1 Race Until 2021," *Motorsport,* April 23, 2007, http://news.bbc.co.uk/sport2/hi/motorsport/formula_one/6583387.stm

FURTHER READING

Books

Blomquist, Christopher. *A Primary Source Guide to Turkey. Countries of the World: A Primary Source Journey.* New York: The Rosen Publishing Group, Inc., 2005.

Davenport, John. *A Brief Political and Geographic History of the Middle East: Where Are Persia, Babylon, and the Ottoman Empire?* Hockessin, DE: Mitchell Lane Publishers, 2007.

Fontes, Justine and Ron. *The Trojan Horse: The Fall of Troy: A Greek Legend.* New York: Graphic Universe, 2007.

Ganeri, Anita. *Focus on Turkey.* Milwaukee, WI: World Almanac Library, 2007.

Lilly, Alexandra. *Teens in Turkey.* Minneapolis, MN: Compass Point Books, 2008.

Works Consulted

This book is based on the author's correspondence with Kayleigh Arslan, a Middle Eastern scholar and the wife of Ercüment Arslan, a native of Turkey, and on the following sources:

Aran, Lale Surmen, and Tankut Aran. *Rick Steves' Istanbul.* Emeryville, Calif.: Avalon Travel Publishing, 2007.

"Armenia and Turkey Normalise Ties." BBC News, October 10, 2009. http://news.bbc.co.uk/2/hi/8299712.stm

"Atatürk and the Modernization of Turkey." American Türk, October 29, 2005. http://americanturk.blogspot.com/2005/10/turkish-republic-was-declared-in-1923.html

Balter, Michael. *The Goddess and the Bull, Çatalhöyük: An Archaeological Journey to the Dawn of Civilization.* New York: Free Press, 2005.

BBC News: Turkey Country Profile http://news.bbc.co.uk/2/hi/europe/country_profiles/1022222.stm#facts

Brosnahan, Tom. Turkey Travel Planner. http://www.turkeytravelplanner.com/

Goodwin, Jason. *Lords of the Horizons: A History of the Ottoman Empire.* New York: Picador, 1998.

Kerper, Barrie, editor. *Istanbul: The Collected Traveler.* New York: A Vintage Departures Original, 2009.

Kinross, Lord, and the editors of the Newsweek Book Division. *Hagia Sophia.* New York: Newsweek Book Division, 1972.

MacLean, Rory. *Magic Bus: On the Hippie Trail from Istanbul to India.* New York: Ig Publishing, 2009.

McDonagh, Bernard, with Dr. M. Naim Turfan. *Blue Guide Turkey, The Aegean and Mediterranean Coasts.* London: A & C Black (Publishers) Limited, 1989.

McPherson, Charlotte. *Culture Smart! Turkey.* Great Britain: Kuperard, Revised Edition 2008.

The National Press: "The National War of Independence." http://www.historyofturkey.com/independence/

Romm, James. *Herodotus.* New Haven, CT: Yale University, 1998.

Sansal, Burak. "Turkish Oil Wrestling." All About Turkey. http://www.allaboutturkey.com/yagligures.htm

Swan, Suzanne, et al. *Eyewitness Travel: Turkey.* New York: DK Publishing, Revised Edition 2010.

On the Internet

CIA—*The World Factbook,* "Turkey" https://www.cia.gov/library/publications/the-world-factbook/geos/tu.html

Grand Bazaar, Istanbul http://www.grandbazaaristanbul.org/Grand_Bazaar_Istanbul.html

Kids Konnect: Turkey http://www.kidskonnect.com/subject-index/26-countriesplaces/393-turkey.html

Turkey Facts and Pictures http://kids.nationalgeographic.com/kids/places/find/turkey/

Turkish Embassy http://www.washington.emb.mfa.gov.tr/default.aspx

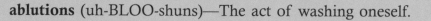

GLOSSARY

ablutions (uh-BLOO-shuns)—The act of washing oneself.

autonomy (aw-TAH-nuh-mee)—The right to self-government.

caliph (KAL-if)—The chief Muslim civil and religious ruler.

creed (KREED)—A statement of faith.

criteria (kry-TEER-ee-yuh)—Standards by which something can be judged.

cuneiform (KYOO-nuh-form)—Relating to the wedge-shaped characters used in many ancient writing systems.

deficit (DEH-fuh-sit)—The amount by which something, like a sum of money, is too small.

enclave (ON-klayv)—A portion of territory surrounded by a larger territory.

executive (ek-ZEK-yoo-tiv)—A person or group that has the power to put plans, actions, or laws into effect.

famine (FAM-in)—An extreme shortage of food.

heretic (HAYR-uh-tik)—A person who believes something that does not agree with what is generally accepted, especially when it comes to religious beliefs.

hieroglyphics (hy-roh-GLIH-fiks)—Writing that consists of pictures.

mandatory (MAN-duh-tor-ee)—Required by law.

persecution (pur-suh-KYOO-shun)—Oppressing or harassing people based on things like their beliefs or race.

polygamy (pah-LIH-guh-mee)—Having more than one husband or wife at the same time.

stagnate (STAG-nayt)—To stop flowing or developing.

sultanate (SUL-tih-nit)—A country or territory ruled by a sultan.

vassal state (VAH-sul STAYT)—A state that is ruled by another state.

veto (VEE-toh)—To reject a decision made by a law-making body.

Amelia LaRoche has written three other books for Mitchell Lane Publishers, including *The Chimaera*, about a mythical beast whose origins are thought to lie in ancient Lycia, a region in today's southern Turkey. She is also the author of *Recipe and Craft Guide to France* and *How to Convince Your Parents You Can Care for a Pet Parrot*. She lives in New England.